I0814849

DISCOVERING THE UNITED STATES

Arkansas

BY IB LARSEN

Kids Core

An Imprint of Abdo Publishing
abdobooks.com

abdobooks.com

Printed in China.
052024
092024

Cover Photo: Sean Pavone/Shutterstock Images
Interior Photos: Shutterstock Images, 4–5, 7 (bottom left), 22, 23, 28 (top right); Steve Byland/Shutterstock Images, 7 (top left); Derek Broussard/iStockphoto, 7 (top right); Levon Avagyan/Shutterstock Images, 7 (bottom right); iStockphoto, 9; Vince Dillion/Oklahoma Historical Society/Archive Photos/Getty Images, 10–11; benoitb/DigitalVision Vectors/Getty Images, 12; Bill Barksdale/Design Pics Inc/Alamy, 14; Wesley Hitt/Getty Images Sport/Getty Images, 16; Eduardo Medrano/Shutterstock Images, 18–19; dlewis33/E+/Getty Images, 20; YP Studio/Shutterstock Images, 21; Nina Alizada/Shutterstock Images, 24; Don Smetzer/Alamy, 26; Red Line Editorial, 28 (top left), 29; Steve Lagreca/Shutterstock Images, 28 (bottom)

Editor: Christa Kelly
Series Designer: Katharine Hale

Library of Congress Control Number: 2023949214

Publisher's Cataloging-in-Publication Data

Names: Larsen, Ib, author.
Title: Arkansas / by Ib Larsen
Description: Minneapolis, Minnesota: Abdo Publishing, 2025 | Series: Discovering the United States | Includes online resources and index.
Identifiers: ISBN 9781098293741 (lib. bdg.) | ISBN 9798384913016 (ebook)
Subjects: LCSH: U.S. states--Juvenile literature. | Arkansas--History--Juvenile literature. | Southeastern States--Juvenile literature. | Physical geography--United States--Juvenile literature.
Classification: DDC 973--dc23

All population data taken from:
"Estimates of Population by Sex, Race, and Hispanic Origin: April 1, 2020 to July 1, 2022." *US Census Bureau, Population Division*, June 2023, census.gov.

CONTENTS

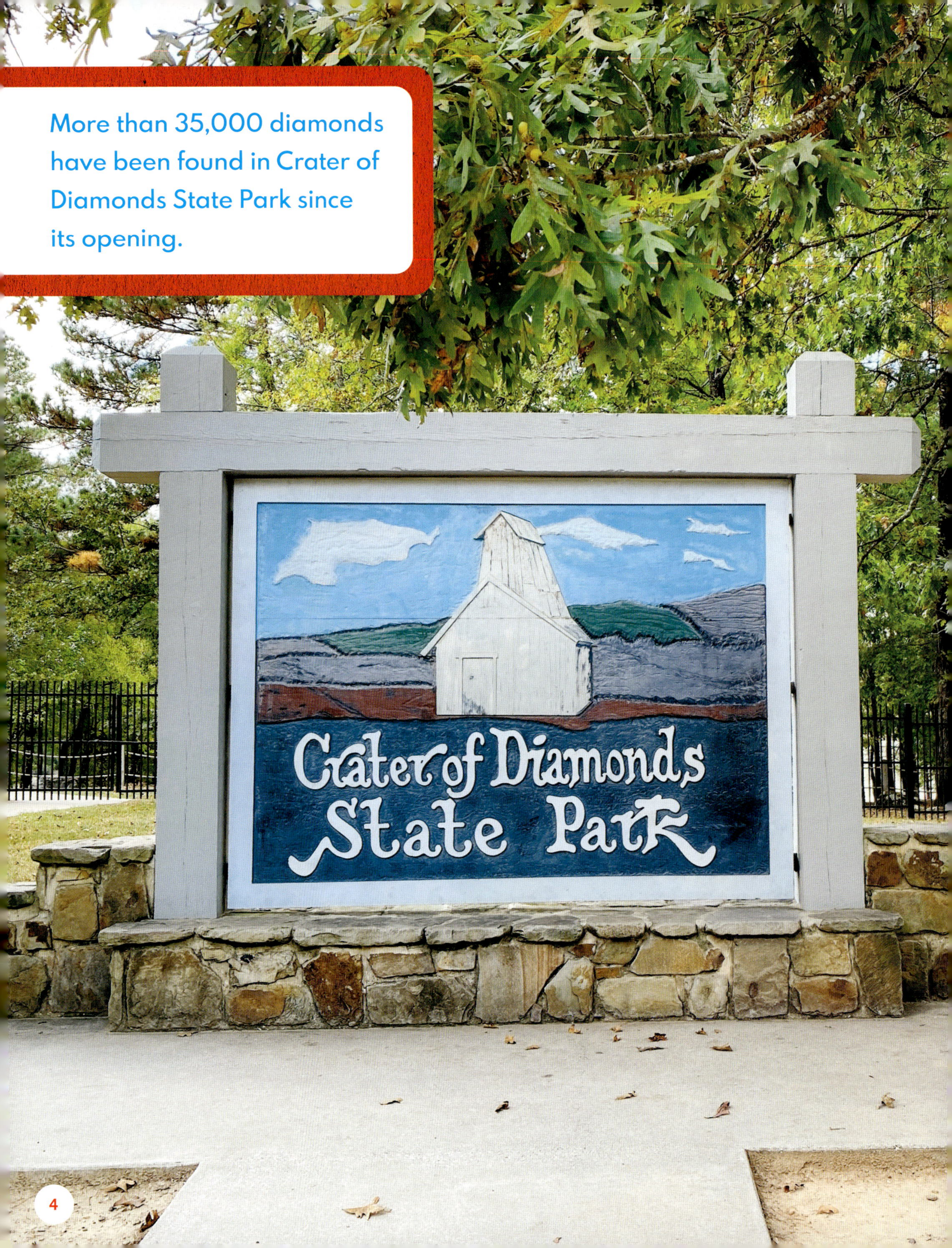

More than 35,000 diamonds have been found in Crater of Diamonds State Park since its opening.

CHAPTER 1

The Uncle Sam Diamond

It was 1924 in a mine in southwestern Arkansas. Wesley O. Basham was spraying down **ore**. A flash in the ore caught his eye. It was a diamond! This was the biggest diamond ever found in the mine. Word of Basham's discovery quickly spread.

The diamond became known as Uncle Sam, after Basham's nickname. One hundred years later, it remained the largest diamond ever found in the United States.

In 1972, the State of Arkansas bought the mine and turned it into Crater of Diamonds State Park. The park is one of the only public diamond-mining sites in the world. Visitors can search for diamonds and keep any that they find. People from all over the United States come to the park for a chance to find the next big diamond.

Arkansas's Land

Arkansas is in the region of the United States called the South. It is a **landlocked** state.

Arkansas Facts

DATE OF STATEHOOD
June 15, 1836

CAPITAL
Little Rock

POPULATION
3,045,637

AREA
53,179 square miles
(137,733 sq km)

STATE BIRD

Northern mockingbird

STATE TREE

Pine

STATE FLOWER

Apple blossom

STATE GEM

Diamond

Each US state has a different population, size, and capital city. States also have state symbols.

Arkansas is bordered by Louisiana to the south and Missouri to the north. To the west are Oklahoma and Texas. To the east, the Mississippi River separates the state from Tennessee and Mississippi.

The northwestern half of the state has tall mountains, including the Ouachita Mountains and the Ozarks. The southeastern half of the state lies closer to sea level. The land there is good for farming.

More than half of Arkansas is covered in forests. The forests are filled with hickory, oak, and pine trees. This land provides homes for white-tailed deer, bald eagles, and black bears.

Arkansas's climate varies depending on **elevation**. In the mountains to the northwest,

Tornadoes

Arkansas gets a lot of tornadoes. The strongest tornado ever recorded in Arkansas was in 1929. It destroyed the town of Sneed and killed 43 people.

The Ozarks cover 13,000 square miles (34,000 sq km) in Arkansas.

temperatures are cooler, and it rains more. In the lowlands to the southeast, temperatures are hotter.

Further Evidence

Look at the website below. Does it give any new evidence to support Chapter One?

Arkansas

abdocorelibrary.com/discovering-arkansas

The Osage people hunted in northwestern Arkansas.

CHAPTER 2

The People of Arkansas

The first people came to Arkansas about 14,000 years ago. They hunted and gathered their food. Over time, nations emerged. These included the Osage, the Caddo, and the Quapaw. The Quapaw and the Caddo farmed.

Hernando de Soto lived from 1496 to 1542.

They grew corn, beans, and other crops. The Osage relied mainly on hunting.

The first European to explore Arkansas was Hernando de Soto. The king of Spain sent de Soto to explore and **settle** the area. Later, France claimed the territory and held it until the United States bought the land in 1803.

Over the next 50 years, the US government forced tens of thousands of American Indians in Arkansas and the surrounding states to resettle farther west. Many died along the way. This removal is known as the Trail of Tears.

Many early Arkansas settlers came from eastern states. Most had Scottish, Irish, or English heritage. Black people were enslaved in Arkansas until the end of the American Civil War (1861–1865). In 1860, about 25 percent of the state's population was Black.

Today, the Black population has shrunk to 15.6 percent. About 71 percent of people in Arkansas are white, 8.6 percent are Hispanic or Latino, 1.8 percent are Asian, and 1.1 percent are American Indian or Alaska Natives.

On average, nearly 60,000 people attend each University of Arkansas Razorbacks football game.

Culture

Food is an important part of Arkansas's culture. **Hush puppies** and coleslaw are two popular Southern foods enjoyed in the state. But some of the best food is found during parties. Sometimes locals throw parties called fish fries. They serve guests fried catfish.

Sports are another important part of life in Arkansas. The University of Arkansas Razorbacks football team attracts thousands of fans at home games. The Arkansas State Red Wolves also has a large fan base.

Walmart

The first Walmart store opened in Rogers, Arkansas, on July 2, 1962. Founded by Sam Walton, the business grew fast. In 2001, Walmart became the largest corporation in the world. Walmart is still based in Arkansas. In April 2023, Walmart employed 54,771 people in the state.

Arkansas produces 9 billion pounds (4 billion kg) of rice every year.

Jobs in Arkansas

Many people in Arkansas are farmers. Some raise chickens and turkeys. Many grow crops such as rice, wheat, soybeans, and cotton. Other people have jobs making products. Many make goods out of wood.

Jennifer James is a fourth-generation farmer. She explained the importance of growing rice:

> Arkansas is the largest producer of US rice. . . . It's big for our economy. . . . We rely on the rice farms to support our communities and to provide jobs. . . . [Our rice is] keeping bellies full and keeping bodies healthy.

Source: "Ep. 31 (Jennifer James, Arkansas Rice Farmer)." *Groundwork* from Farm Policy Facts, n.d., farmpolicyfacts.org. Accessed 8 Sep. 2023.

What's the Big Idea?

Read this quote carefully. What is its main idea? Explain how the main idea is supported by details.

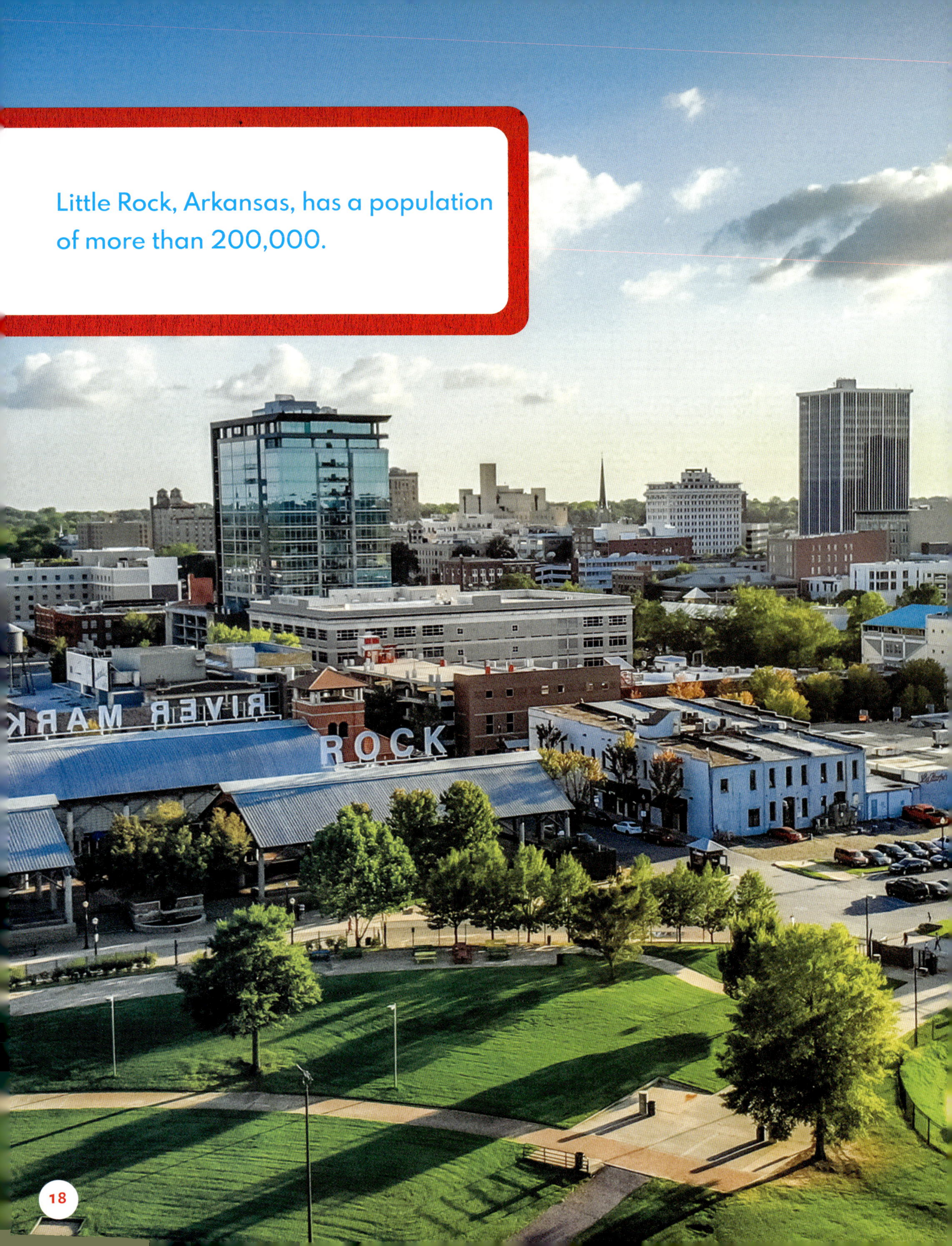

Little Rock, Arkansas, has a population of more than 200,000.

CHAPTER 3

Places in Arkansas

Little Rock is the capital of Arkansas. It is the state's most **populated** city. The city was named after a small rock formation found by a French explorer in 1722. The next two most populated cities in Arkansas are Fayetteville and Fort Smith.

The current Arkansas flag was created in 1924.

Parks

Hot Springs National Park is Arkansas's only national park. The park is named after the hot

The springs at Hot Springs National Park average a temperature of 143 degrees Fahrenheit (62°C).

water that comes out of the ground. Water sinks deep underground, where it is very hot. The water heats up and returns to the surface. This process takes 4,000 years. Visitors can camp at the park and hike its trails.

Pinnacle Mountain State Park is located to the west of Little Rock.

Arkansas has many state parks for visitors to enjoy. Pinnacle Mountain State Park has exciting mountain biking trails. At Lake Catherine State Park, visitors can rent cabins and take boats out on the lake.

Lake Catherine State Park is in the Ouachita Mountains.

A monument in front of Arkansas's capitol building honors the Little Rock Nine.

Landmarks

Arkansas is home to many important landmarks. Visitors to the state capital can see Little Rock Central High School. In 1957, nine Black students were admitted to the school. Until then, only white students were allowed in the school. The students were threatened by soldiers and people from across the country. But the students went to the school anyway.

There are also many natural landmarks in Arkansas. In the northern part of the state, the Blanchard Springs Caverns stretch for miles underground. The caves are made of limestone. They are more than 300 million years old.

The Little Rock Nine

The nine Black students who attended Little Rock Central High School in 1957 were called the Little Rock Nine. Some of them, such as Carlotta Walls LaNier and Melba Pattillo Beals, wrote books about their experiences at the school.

New stalactites and stalagmites are still forming in the Blanchard Springs Caverns.

The area is sacred to the Osage nation. Today, visitors come to Blanchard Springs Caverns to see the cave's **stalactites** and **stalagmites**. Tour guides lead hikes through the caverns and teach visitors about how caves form.

Mount Magazine, Arkansas's tallest mountain, is another popular landmark. Visitors can climb the mountain and camp nearby. Some go horseback riding.

Arkansas has a fascinating history, delicious food, and beautiful landmarks. Visitors can enjoy the natural beauty of its many parks, eat catfish, or watch a game of football. There's something for everyone in the state of Arkansas!

Explore Online

Visit the website below. Does it give any new information about Hot Springs National Park that wasn't in Chapter Three?

Hot Springs National Park

abdocorelibrary.com/discovering-arkansas

State Map

KEY

 Capital

 Park

City or town

Point of interest

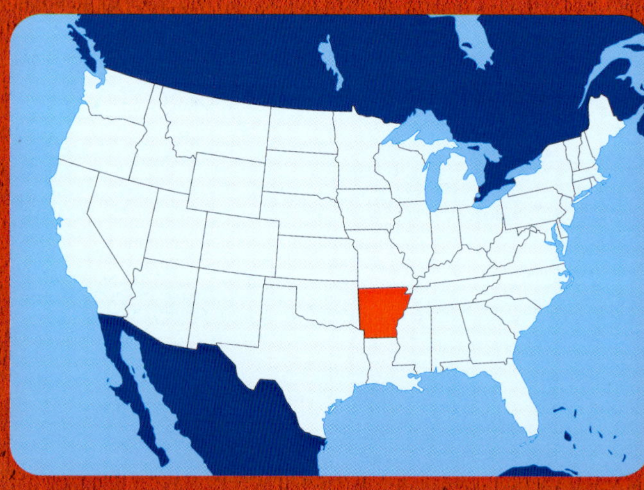

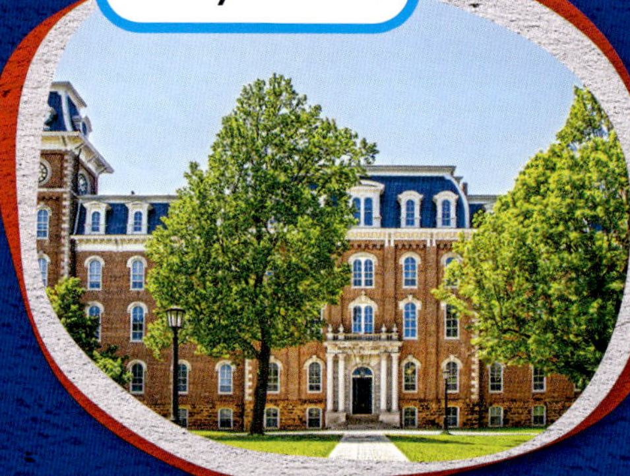

University of Arkansas in Fayetteville

Devil's Den State Park

Arkansas: The Natural State

Glossary

elevation
the height above sea level

hush puppies
a dish made by deep-frying cornmeal batter

landlocked
describing an area that is entirely surrounded by land

ore
a rock containing valuable minerals

populated
settled or lived in

settle
to move into a new area

stalactites
icicle-shaped rock formations that hang from cave ceilings

stalagmites
icicle-shaped rock formations that rise from cave floors

Online Resources

To learn more about Arkansas, visit our free resource websites below.

Visit **abdocorelibrary.com** or scan this QR code for free Common Core resources for teachers and students, including vetted activities, multimedia, and booklinks, for deeper subject comprehension.

Visit **abdobooklinks.com** or scan this QR code for free additional online weblinks for further learning. These links are routinely monitored and updated to provide the most current information available.

Learn More

Hall, Ashley, and Lee Hall. *Gems for Kids.* Rockridge, 2021.

Payne, Stefanie. *The National Parks.* DK, 2020.

Tieck, Sarah. *Arkansas.* Abdo, 2020.

Index

About the Author

Ib Larsen is a writer and editorial assistant living in Saint Paul, Minnesota.